M000104917

Arsenal FC Quiz Book

101 Questions That Will Test Your Knowledge of the Gunners

Published by Glowworm Press
7 Nuffield Way
Abingdon OX14 1RL

By Chris Carpenter

Arsenal Football Club

This book contains one hundred and one informative and entertaining trivia questions with multiple choice answers. With 101 questions, some easy, some more challenging, this book will test your knowledge and memory of the club's long and successful history. The book is packed with information and is a must-have for all loyal Gooners.

You will be asked many fun and interesting questions on a wide range of topics associated with the Gunners for you to test yourself. You will be quizzed on players, legends, managers, opponents, transfer deals, trophies, records, honours, fixtures, songs and more, guaranteeing you both an educational experience and plenty of fun. This Arsenal Quiz Book is great entertainment for Gunners fans of all ages, and will test your knowledge of **Arsenal Football Club**'s proud history.

2020/21 Season Edition

FOREWORD

When I was asked to write a foreword to this book I was flattered.

I have known the author Chris Carpenter for many years and his knowledge of facts and figures is phenomenal.

His love for football and his skill in writing quiz books make him the ideal man to pay homage to my great love Arsenal Football Club.

This book came about as a result of a challenge in a Lebanese restaurant of all places!

I do hope you enjoy the book.

Colin Williams

Let's start with some relatively easy questions.

1. When was Arsenal founded?
   A. 1884
   B. 1886
   C. 1888

2. What is Arsenal's nickname?
   A. The Alberts
   B. The Gunners
   C. The Hammers

3. Where does Arsenal play their home games?
   A. Emirates Stadium
   B. Etihad Stadium
   C. Qatari Stadium

4. What is the stadium's capacity?
   A. 60,047
   B. 60,470
   C. 60,704

5. Who or what is the club mascot?
   A. Fred the Red
   B. Gunnersaurus
   C. Tyrannosaurus

6. Who has made the most appearances for the club in total?
   A. Tony Adams

B. Thierry Henry
C. David O'Leary

7. Who is the club's record goal scorer?
   A. Cliff Bastin
   B. Thierry Henry
   C. Ian Wright

8. Who scored the fastest ever goal by a substitute for the club?
   A. Nicklas Bendtner
   B. Alan Sunderland
   C. Theo Walcott

9. Which of the following songs do the players run out to?
   A. Go West
   B. The Macarena
   C. The Wonder Of You

10. Which of these is a well known pub near the ground?
    A. The Ten Bridges
    B. The Eleven Lords
    C. The Twelve Pins

OK, so here are the answers to the first ten questions. If you get eight or more right, you are doing well, but don't get too cocky, as the questions do get harder.

A1. Arsenal was founded in October 1886 by a group of workers at Royal Arsenal, an armaments factory. Originally formed as Dial Square, which was the heart of the Royal Arsenal complex, the club took the name of the whole complex just a month later.

A2. Arsenal's nickname is of course the Gunners.

A3. Arsenal play their home games at the Emirates Stadium, named after Emirates Airlines who acquired the naming rights to the stadium.

A4. According to the Wikipedia page on the stadium itself, the current stadium capacity is 60,704. The stadium is the fourth largest football stadium in England.

A5. The club mascot is the one and only Gunnersaurus.

A6. David O'Leary has made the most appearances for the club. He played in 722 first team matches in total. Legend.

A7. Thierry Henry is Arsenal's record goal scorer with 228 goals.

A8. Oh Lord. Just six seconds after coming off the bench, Nicklas Bendtner scored against Tottenham Hotspur on 22nd December 2007.

A9. The players run out onto the pitch with Elvis Presley singing "The Wonder Of You".

A10. The Twelve Pins is a well known pub located just under a mile away from the ground. Be prepared to queue for a pint though. Perhaps the nearest pub is The Tollington, so give yourself a bonus point if you knew that.

OK, back to the questions.

11. What is the highest number of goals that Arsenal has scored in a league season?
   A. 123
   B. 125
   C. 127

12. What is the fewest number of goals that Arsenal has conceded in a league season?
   A. 14
   B. 17
   C. 20

13. Who has scored the most penalties for the club?
   A. Thierry Henry
   B. Robin van Persie
   C. Ian Wright

14. Who has made the most league appearances for the club?
   A. Tony Adams
   B. Thierry Henry
   C. David O'Leary

15. In which end of the stadium is the famous Arsenal clock?
   A. East End
   B. North End
   C. South End

16. What is the name of the club's previous stadium?
    A. Finsbury
    B. Highbury
    C. Hornsey

17. What is the club's record attendance?
    A. 73,013
    B. 73,295
    C. 73,707

18. Where is Arsenal's training ground?
    A. Carrington
    B. Cobham
    C. London Colney

19. What is the capacity of the upper tier of the Emirates Stadium?
    A. 25,230
    B. 26,646
    C. 27,402

20. What is the size of the pitch?
    A. 105x70 metres
    B. 105x68 metres
    C. 105x62 metres

Here are the answers to the last set of questions.

A11. Arsenal scored 127 goals in 42 matches in the 1930/31 season.

A12. Arsenal conceded just 17 goals in 38 matches in the 1998/99 season.

A13. Thierry Henry holds the record for the most penalties scored for the club. He scored 22 spot kicks.

A14. It's that man David O'Leary again. With 558 league appearances, he holds the record for the most league appearances for the club.

A15. The Arsenal clock is at the South End of the Emirates Stadium.

A16. Highbury was Arsenal's home stadium from September 1913 until May 2006.

A17. Arsenal's record home attendance at Highbury was 73,295 against Sunderland on the 9th March 1935. However, Arsenal played their Champions League home games at Wembley for a couple of seasons, and on 25th November 1998 73,707 fans watched the team play against French side RC Lens.

A18. The Arsenal training ground is located at London Colney, a village near St Albans in Hertfordshire.

A19. 26,646 fans can sit in the upper tier of the Emirates Stadium. All seated; and all in comfort too.

A20. The pitch is 105 metres long and 68 metres wide.

Now we move onto some questions about the club's records.

21. What is the club's record win in the league?
    A. 10-0
    B. 12-0
    C. 14-0

22. Who did they beat?
    A. Loughborough
    B. Peterborough
    C. Middlesbrough

23. In which season?
    A. 1896/1897
    B. 1899/1900
    C. 1902/1903

24. What is the club's record win in European competition?
    A. 6-0
    B. 7-0
    C. 8-0

25. Who did they beat?
    A. CSKA Moscow
    B. Slavia Prague
    C. Standard Liege

26. What is the club's record defeat?

A. 0-7
B. 0-8
C. 0-9

27. Who against?
    A. Loughborough
    B. Middlesbrough
    C. Peterborough

28. What were Arsenal known as in the 1930s?
    A. The Bank of England club
    B. The Investors club
    C. The Stockbrokers club

29. Who has scored the most hat tricks for Arsenal?
    A. Jimmy Brain
    B. Ted Drake
    C. Jack Lambert

30. What is the club's official twitter account?
    A. @Arsenal
    B. @ArsenalFC
    C. @OfficialArsenal

Here is the latest set of answers.

A21. The club's record win in the league is 12-0. They have also won 7-0 twice in the Premier League era.

A22. Arsenal beat Loughborough 12-0.

A23. The match took place in a Second Division match on 12th March 1900, so it was during the 1899/1900 season.

A24. The club's record win in European competition is 7-0.

A25. Arsenal have beaten both Standard Liege and Slavia Prague 7-0 in European competitions. Give yourself a bonus point if you knew that.

A27. The club's record defeat in any competition is 0-8.

A28. Loughborough defeated Arsenal 8-0, a long, long time ago. The match was played on 12th December 1896, in the 1896/97 season.

A29. The name "Bank of England club" came about after the record-breaking spending of Arsenal in the 1930s. Arsenal's new home in Highbury provided them with considerable resources, such that, in 1935, they became the first club to earn over £100,000 from gate receipts. Accompanied by £2,500 earned from match day programme sales and financial reserves of over £60,000, the "Bank of England club" moniker became regularly used to describe Arsenal. It was also used to refer to the perceived grandeur of Arsenal's surroundings after the 1930s construction of Highbury's Art Deco stands and terrazzo marbled halls.

A30. @Arsenal is the club's official twitter account. It tweets multiple times daily and the account now has over 16 million followers.

Now we move onto questions about the club's trophies.

31. When did the club win their first league title?
    A. 1910/11
    B. 1920/21
    C. 1930/31

32. When did the club win their first FA Cup?
    A. 1926/27
    B. 1929/30
    C. 1932/33

33. Who did they beat in the final?
    A. Huddersfield Town
    B. Ipswich Town
    C. Luton Town

34. What was the score?
    A. 1-0
    B. 2-0
    C. 3-0

35. How many times have Arsenal won the League?
    A. 9
    B. 11
    C. 13

36. How many times have Arsenal won the
    FA Cup?
    A. 12
    B. 13
    C. 14

37. How many times have Arsenal won the
    League Cup?
    A. 1
    B. 2
    C. 3

38. Who was the last captain to lift the
    League trophy?
    A. Tony Adams
    B. Mikel Arteta
    C. Patrick Vieira

39. Who was the last captain to lift the FA
    Cup?
    A. Pierre-Emerick Aubameyang
    B. Per Mertesacker
    C. Thomas Vermaelen

40. Who was the last captain to lift the
    League Cup?
    A. Tony Adams
    B. William Gallas
    C. Thierry Henry

Here is the latest set of answers.

A31. Arsenal won their first League title at the end of the 1930/31 season.

A32. Arsenal won their first FA Cup at the end of the 1929/30 season.

A33. Arsenal defeated Huddersfield Town at Wembley Stadium on 26th April 1930 in front of 92,488 spectators.

A34. Arsenal won 2-0, with goals from Alex James and Jack Lambert.

A35. Arsenal have won the League 13 times (1930/31, 1932/33, 1933/34, 1934/35, 1937/38, 1947/48, 1952/53, 1970/71, 1988/89, 1990/91, 1997/98, 2001/02 and 2003/04).

A36. Arsenal have won the FA Cup a record 14 times (1930, 1936, 1950, 1971, 1979, 1993, 1998, 2002, 2003, 2005, 2014, 2015, 2017 and 2020).

A37. Arsenal have won the League Cup twice (1987 and 1993).

A38. Patrick Vieira was the last captain to lift the League trophy. He lifted the trophy at the end of the 2003/04 season.

A39. Pierre-Emerick Aubameyang was the last captain to lift the FA Cup. He lifted the cup when Arsenal defeated Chelsea 2-1 at Wembley Stadium on 1st August 2020.

A40. Tony Adams was the last captain to lift the League Cup, back in the 1992/93 season. He lifted the cup after Arsenal defeated Sheffield Wednesday 2-1 in the final, in what was the first of three Wembley matches between the two sides that season. Arsenal and Wednesday also met in the FA Cup Final of that season, which went to a replay.

I hope you're getting most of the answers right. Let's move onto the next set of questions.

41. What is the record transfer fee paid by Arsenal?
    A. £52 million
    B. £62 million
    C. £72 million

42. Who was the record transfer fee paid for?
    A. Pierre-Emerick Aubameyang
    B. Mesut Özil
    C. Nicolas Pepe

43. What is the record transfer fee received by the club?
    A. £30 million
    B. £35 million
    C. £40 million

44. Who was the record transfer fee received for?
    A. Nicolas Anelka
    B. Cesc Fàbregas
    C. Alex Oxlade-Chamberlain

45. Who was the first Arsenal player to play for England?
    A. Jimmy Ashcroft

B. Dave Bowen
C. Caesar Jenkyns

46. Who has won the most international caps whilst an Arsenal player?
   A. Yossi Benayoun
   B. Thierry Henry
   C. Patrick Vieira

47. Who has scored the most international goals whilst an Arsenal player?
   A. Andrei Arshavin
   B. Thierry Henry
   C. Robin van Persie

48. Who is the youngest player ever to represent the club?
   A. Cesc Fàbregas
   B. Ted Drake
   C. Theo Walcott

49. Who is the youngest ever goalscorer?
   A. Cesc Fàbregas
   B. Robin van Persie
   C. Theo Walcott

50. Who is the oldest player ever to represent the club?
   A. Ted Drake
   B. Jock Rutherford
   C. David Seaman

Here is the latest set of answers.

A41. Arsenal's record transfer fee paid is £72 million.

A42. Arsenal paid French club Lille £72 million for Nicolas Pepe in July 2019. This beat the previous record of £55 million paid to Borussia Dortmund for Pierre-Emerick Aubameyang in January 2018.

A43. The record transfer fee received by Arsenal is £40 million.

A44. The fee was received from Liverpool for Alex Oxlade-Chamberlain in August 2017.

A45. Jimmy Ashcroft was the first Arsenal player to play for England. He appeared against Ireland on 17th February 1906.

A46. Thierry Henry won 81 of his 123 caps for France while he was at Arsenal.

A47. Thierry Henry scored the most international goals whilst an Arsenal player.

A48. Cesc Fàbregas is the youngest player ever to represent the club. He made his first team appearance at the age of just 16 years and 177 days old on 28th October 2003 in a League Cup match against Rotherham.

A49. Fàbregas is also the youngest ever goal scorer. He scored against Wolverhampton Wanderers in a League Cup game on 2nd December 2003, when he was just 16 years, 212 days old.

A50. Jock Rutherford is the oldest player ever to represent the club. He appeared for the club aged 41 years 159 days in a game against Manchester City in the old First Division on 20th March 1926.

I hope you're learning some new facts about the Gunners.

51. Who is Arsenal's oldest ever goal scorer?
    A. Cliff Bastin
    B. Ted Drake
    C. Jock Rutherford

52. Who is the club's longest serving post war manager?
    A. George Allison
    B. George Graham
    C. Arsène Wenger

53. Who is the club's longest serving manager of all time?
    A. Herbert Chapman
    B. Thomas Mitchell
    C. Arsène Wenger

54. What is the name of the Arsenal match day programme?
    A. The Arsenal
    B. The Gunners
    C. The Official Matchday Programme

55. When did Arsenal win the European Cup Winners' Cup?
    A. 1992
    B. 1994
    C. 1996

56. Which of these is an Arsenal fanzine?
   A. Red Army
   B. The Gooner
   C. The Gunner

57. What motif is on the club crest?
   A. A cannon
   B. A gun
   C. A lion

58. What is the club's motto?
   A. Consilio et Labore
   B. Superbia in Proelia
   C. Victoria Concordia Crescit

59. Who is considered as Arsenal's main rivals?
   A. Manchester United
   B. Tottenham Hotspur
   C. West Ham United

60. Which of these is a popular fan's chant?
   A. Arsenal, we're on your side
   B. Ooh to be a Gooner
   C. Red is the colour

Here is the latest set of answers.

A51. Jock Rutherford is Arsenal's oldest ever goal scorer. He scored against Sheffield United at the age of 39 years, 352 days on 20th September 1924.

A52. Arsène Wenger is the club's longest serving post war manager. A lot of people clearly trusted him.

A53. Arsène Wenger is the club's longest serving manager of all time. He was in the post from 1st October 1996 until 13th May 2018.

A54. The name of the Arsenal match day programme is The Official Matchday Programme.

A55. Arsenal won the European Cup Winners' Cup in 1994, beating Parma 1-0 in the final in Copenhagen on 4th May 1994 with the goal scored by Alan Smith.

A56. The Gooner is probably the best known of the Arsenal fanzines and it has a popular website too at onlinegooner.com

A57. Arsenal's crest consists of a cannon. The club crest has evolved a lot over the years, and the current crest has been used since 2002.

A58. The Latin motto of Arsenal is 'Victoria Concordia Crescit'. It means 'Victory through Harmony' in English.

A59. Tottenham are of course Arsenal's main rival.

A60. "Ooh to be a Gooner" is a well-known fan's chant. It's breathtakingly simple yet extraordinarily catchy.

Let's give you some easier questions.

61. What is the traditional colour of the home shirt?
    A. Blue with white sleeves
    B. Red with white sleeves
    C. White with red sleeves

62. What is the traditional colour of the away shirt?
    A. Yellow
    B. Blue
    C. White

63. Who is the current club sponsor?
    A. Emirates
    B. Etihad
    C. Gulf Air

64. Who was the first club sponsor?
    A. Dreamcast
    B. JVC
    C. Sega

65. Which of these telecom companies once sponsored the club?
    A. Orange
    B. O2
    C. Vodafone

66. Who is currently the club chairman?

A. Peter Hill-Wood
B. Chips Keswick
C. Stan Kroenke

67. Who was the first band to play a concert at the Emirates Stadium?
    A. Coldplay
    B. Green Day
    C. Bruce Springsteen

68. Who was the club's first black player?
    A. Brendan Batson
    B. Paul Canoville
    C. Tony Whelan

69. Who was the club's first ever match in the league against?
    A. Manchester United
    B. Newcastle United
    C. West Ham United

70. Who started the 2020/21 season as manager?
    A. Mikel Arteta
    B. Unai Emery
    C. Pat Rice

Here are the answers to the last set of questions.

A61. The traditional colour of the home shirt is red with white sleeves.

A62. The club has used many different colours for their change of kit, but it is now generally accepted that the traditional colour of the away shirt is yellow.

A63. Emirates Airlines is the current sponsor of Arsenal. They have sponsored the club since 2006. The £100 million deal, when it was signed, was the largest sponsorship deal in the entire history of English football.

A64. JVC was the first sponsor of Arsenal, from 1981 to 1999.

A65. O2 sponsored Arsenal from 2002 until 2006.

A66. Merchant banker Sir Chips Keswick is the current club chairman.

A67. Bruce Springsteen and the E Street Band became the first band to play a concert at the stadium on 30th May 2008.

A68. Brendan Batson was the club's first black player. He joined the club in 1971.

A69. The club's first match in the League was against Newcastle United. The match was played on 2nd September 1893. The match finished in a 2-2 draw.

A70. Mikel Arteta started the 2020/21 season as manager, having been appointed to the job in December 2019.

Here is the next batch of ten questions.

71. When was Arsenal Ladies founded?
    A. 1967
    B. 1977
    C. 1987

72. How many times have Arsenal won the League and FA Cup Double?
    A. 2
    B. 3
    C. 4

73. How many goals did Dennis Bergkamp score for the club?
    A. 120
    B. 125
    C. 130

74. Who was the first Arsenal player to play in a World Cup final?
    A. Thierry Henry
    B. Emmanuel Petit
    C. Patrick Vieira

75. Who was the top goal scorer for the 2019/20 season?
    A. Pierre-Emerick Aubameyang
    B. Alexandre Lacazette
    C. Gabriel Martinelli

76. How many consecutive seasons did Thierry Henry score more than 20 goals in the league?
    A. 3
    B. 4
    C. 5

77. How many times have Arsenal been relegated from the top division?
    A. 0
    B. 1
    C. 2

78. Who is known as "The Professor"?
    A. George Graham
    B. Bertie Mee
    C. Arsene Wenger

79. What is the club's record away win against Spurs?
    A. 4-0
    B. 5-0
    C. 6-0

80. In 1994 how many consecutive games did Ian Wright score in?
    A. 10
    B. 11
    C. 12

A71. Arsenal Ladies was founded in 1987.

A72. Arsenal have won the League and FA Cup double three times. (1971, 1998 and 2002)

A73. Dennis Bergkamp scored 120 goals for Arsenal. Legend.

A74. Emmanuel Petit was the first Arsenal player to play in a World Cup final. He started the game for France in the 1998 World Cup Final in Paris on 12th July 1998. Patrick Vieira came on as a second half substitute.

A75. Pierre-Emerick Aubameyang was the top goal scorer for the 2019/20 season. He scored 29 goals in all competitions, including 22 in The Premier League.

A76. In 2006, Henry became the first player to score more than 20 goals in the league for five consecutive seasons (2001/02 to 2005/06).

A77. Arsenal have been relegated from the top division only once in their history, way back in the 1912/13 season.

A78. Arsene Wenger is known as "The Professor".

A79. The club's record away win against Spurs is 6-0 on 6th March 1935.

A80. During a purple patch between 15th September 1994 and 23rd November 1994, Ian Wright Wright Wright scored in 12 consecutive games, scoring 16 goals in total!

Here is the next set of questions.

81. Who is the youngest ever goal scorer in the FA Cup for Arsenal?
    A. Cliff Bastin
    B. Cesc Fàbregas
    C. Doug Lishman

82. Which year did Arsenal move to the Emirates Stadium?
    A. 2004
    B. 2005
    C. 2006

83. When did Arsenal start wearing white sleeves?
    A. 1923
    B. 1928
    C. 1933

84. Who holds the record for the most consecutive appearances?
    A. George Armstrong
    B. Tom Parker
    C. Ray Parlour

85. What was the name of the 1971 song sung by the team?
    A. Come on Arsenal
    B. Good old Arsenal
    C. Up the Arsenal

86. Who was the first ever full time
    manager of Arsenal?
        A. George Graham
        B. Graham Rix
        C. Thomas Mitchell

87. What was the transfer fee received for
    Alex Iwobi?
        A. £25 million
        B. £30 million
        C. £35 million

88. Who is the youngest ever scorer of a
    hat-trick for the club?
        A. Cliff Bastin
        B. Joe Hulme
        C. John Radford

89. Who was the first Arsenal player to be
    sent off at the Emirates Stadium?
        A. Nicolas Anelka
        B. Marc Overmars
        C. Philippe Senderos

90. When was George Graham appointed as
    manager of Arsenal?
        A. 1980
        B. 1983
        C. 1986

Here are the answers to the latest set of questions.

A81. Cliff Bastin is the youngest ever goal scorer in the FA Cup for Arsenal. He scored at the age of 17 years 303 days against Chelsea on 11th January 1930.

A82. Arsenal moved to the Emirates Stadium in 2006.

A83. Arsenal started wearing shirts with white sleeves in 1933. Depending on which source you believe, the 'Great Innovator' Herbert Chapman either noticed someone at the ground wearing a red sleeveless sweater over a white shirt or he played golf with the famous cartoonist of the day Tom Webster, who wore something similar. Either way, the 'look' inspired the manager to create a new strip combining a red shirt with white collar and sleeves

A84. With 172 appearances, Tom Parker holds the record for the most consecutive appearances for the club. He appeared consecutively from 3rd April 1926 to 26th December 1929.

A85. "Good Old Arsenal" was performed by Arsenal's first team squad as their 1971 FA

Cup Final song. This was the first record ever released to be performed by a football team's squad to commemorate their reaching the FA Cup Final. Football pundit Jimmy Hill wrote the words to the song, loosely based upon the tune of 'Rule, Britannia!'

A86. Thomas Mitchell was the first ever full time manager of Arsenal.

A87. £35 million was received for selling Alex Iwobi to Everton in August 2019.

A88. John Radford is the youngest ever scorer of a hat-trick for the club. He scored it at the tender age of 17 years 315 days against Wolves on 2nd January 1965.

A89. Philippe Senderos was the first Arsenal player to be sent off at the Emirates Stadium, in a Premier League match against Portsmouth on 2nd September 2007.

A90. George Graham joined as manager of Arsenal on 14th May 1986.

Here is the final set of questions. Enjoy!

91. What is the highest number of away goals that Arsenal has scored in a league season?
    A. 80
    B. 60
    C. 72

92. What position did Arsenal finish at the end of the 2019/20 season?
    A. 6th
    B. 7th
    C. 8th

93. Which season did Arsenal reach the final of UEFA Champions League?
    A. 2003/04
    B. 2004/05
    C. 2005/06

94. In what year did Arsenal first use numbers on their shirts?
    A. 1926
    B. 1927
    C. 1928

95. Who scored the most goals in a season for the club?
    A. Ted Drake
    B. Thierry Henry

C. Alan Smith

96. Where was Bernd Leno born?
    A. Austria
    B. Germany
    C. Italy

97. What shirt number does Kieran Tierney wear?
    A. 3
    B. 13
    C. 23

98. Which Arsenal legend is nick named as "Titi"?
    A. Thierry Henry
    B. Thomas Vermaelen
    C. Patrick Vieira

99. During which season did the players wear a redcurrant coloured home shirt?
    A. 2004/05
    B. 2005/06
    C. 2006/07

100. What is the club's official website address?
    A. Arsenal.com
    B. ArsenalFC.com
    C. Arsenalfc.co.uk

101. Which manager has a bronze statue
outside the Emirates Stadium?
- A. Herbert Chapman
- B. Don Howe
- C. Arsene Wenger

Here is the final set of answers.

A91. The highest number of away goals that Arsenal has scored in a league season is 60 in the 1930/31 season.

A92. Arsenal finished the 2019/20 season in 8th position.

A93. Arsenal reached the final of the UEFA Champions League at the end of the 2005/06 season. Unfortunately Arsenal lost to Barcelona 2-1 in the final.

A94. Arsenal was the first team in the top flight to use shirt numbers during a game. They did this way back in 1927. The innovation came from Herbert Chapman, a man who was many years ahead of his time.

A95. Ted Drake scored the most goals in a season for the club. He scored 44 goals in the 1934/35 season.

A96. Goalkeeper Leno was born in Germany.

A97. Kieran Tierney wears shirt number 3.

A98. Thierry Henry is nicknamed "Titi".

A99. 2005/06 was the final season to be played at Highbury and to commemorate a redcurrant home kit was worn to honour the shirts worn in 1913.

A100. Arsenal.com is the club's official website address.

A101. A bronze statue of innovative manager Herbert Chapman is present outside the Emirates Stadium. Additionally, defensive stalwart Tony Adams, goal scoring hero Thierry Henry and charismatic striker Dennis Bergkamp have also been commemorated in bronze statues outside the stadium.

That's it. That's a great question to finish with. I hope you enjoyed this book, and I hope you got most of the answers right.

I also hope you learnt some new facts about the club, and if you saw anything wrong, or have a general comment, please visit the glowwormpress.com website.

Thanks for reading, and if you did enjoy the book, would you be so kind as leave a positive review on Amazon.

Made in the USA
Las Vegas, NV
17 December 2020